Translation

Fred D'Aguiar was born in London in 1960 to Guyanese parents. He grew up in Guyana, returning to England in his teens. He trained as a psychiatric nurse before reading African and Caribbean Studies at the University of Kent, Canterbury. He was Judith E. Wilson Fellow at Cambridge University and has been shortlisted for the T.S. Eliot Prize. He is also the author of four novels, the first of which, *The Longest Memory* (Pantheon, 1994), won both the David Higham Prize for Fiction and the Whitbread First Novel Award. His plays include *High Life* (1987) and *A Jamaican Airman Foresees His Death* (1991), which was performed at the Royal Court Theatre, London. *Mr Reasonable* was broadcast on BBC Radio 4 in 2015.

Fred D'Aguiar was Judith E. Wilson Fellow at Cambridge University from 1989-90 and has taught in the United States since 1992, where he has been Visiting Writer at Amherst, Massachusetts (1992-4), Assistant Professor of English at Bates College in Lewiston, Maine (1994-5), and Professor of English and Creative Writing at the University of Miami. He was Professor of English and Gloria D. Smith Professor of Africana Studies at Virginia Tech State University. In 2015 he became a Professor of English and Director of Creative Writing at UCLA.

Fred D'Aguiar's poetry books include

Mama Dot (1985)
Airy Hall (1989; winner of the Guyana Poetry Prize)
British Subjects (1993)
Bill of Rights (1998; shortlisted for the T.S. Eliot Prize)
An English Sampler: New and Selected Poems (2001)

and from Carcanet
Continental Shelf (2009; shortlisted for the T.S. Eliot Prize)
The Rose of Toulouse (2013)

For Aniyah

First published in Great Britain in 2018 by
Carcanet Press Ltd
Alliance House, 30 Cross Street
Manchester M2 7AQ
www.carcanet.co.uk

A CIP catalogue record for this book is available from the British Library.
ISBN 978 1 78410 606 5

The publisher acknowledges financial assistance from Arts Council England.

Typeset in England by XL Publishing Services, Exmouth
Printed and bound in England by SRP Ltd, Exeter

FRED D'AGUIAR

Translations from Memory

CARCANET

Contents

Acknowledgements

Tidal emerged out of a residency at Liverpool University English Department's *Travel, Transculturality and Identity in England* (TIDE) project led by Professor Nandini Das, and published in *Transitions* (USA).

The Sirens' Song by Romare Bearden appeared in the anthology *Bearden's Odyssey: Poets Responding to the Art of Romare Bearden*, edited by Kwame Dawes and Matthew Shenoda (Northwestern University, 2017).

Other poems appeared in part or in revised form in the following: *Griffith Review* (Australia), *Faultline* (USA), *Island* (Australia) and *Poetry* (USA).

Museum Gilgamesh

A teen couple, hand-in-hand, breeze past
The senior uniformed greeter and barely glance
One semi-colon, backlit, carved from elephant
Tusk, an intro to the whole, displayed behind glass.

Instead they head for backrooms, where apostrophe,
Tilde, dieresis, look less prized, and shadows invite
These lovers to steal a kiss or two, out of sight,
Or so they think, unaware as they are of security

Cameras discreetly placed in corners to record
All in those quiet rooms. As they head for the exit
The pair approaches a full stop, the last big exhibit,
Mounted as grandly as any finality accords.

Both pray, Sweet Jesus, let this last, but they know
For all their present magic, they must end now.

Greek & Latin

1

A puzzle of perfumed rubble,
Ethnologists in white gloves brush,

label, date and crate, slaves under
laden tables, who bare teeth, force
smiles, for a motion, a wager, tabled
for all seated around – well, yes – High

Table; they look out one eye, named
progress, passed from hand to mouth
to hand, back and forth, as women
enter, exit, Morse code foot shuffle
headdress disguise, fashion muzzle.

2

There is more to race than a tanning
salon suggests. Take our woman in black,
pink gums, pink cuticles, white instep,
her black is seasonal and in your face.

She walks into and out of her skin
as one would a supermarket
without a second thought for
all the things in her shopping

cart: tanning oil, roll-on anti-perspirant,
(begin sax solo) quail, plus sales tax.

Greco-Roman

Poor language, gives away too much
too soon, asks for too little too late,
or else basks in continual deferral?

Peel my dead skin, layer by rusted layer,
watch how limited time reddens, folds
under scrutiny, yields to touch

as much as talk, and looks,
if looks could kill, rather than this blank
silence among dead, this echo in a shared grave.

Homer

The topless towers on South Beach
Keep their shape with a watering can
That stops them crumbing in the sun.

Under the overpass homeless men,
Women and some children stake out
Ground with cardboard and shopping carts.

Armies of tourists snap the castle and stare,
News crews aim and shoot the ramparts
From various angles and interview

The architect – a shy young man
Bronzed like a Greek god with hair
Involuntarily bleached by sun and sea

Dirty blonde and twisted by neglect
Into dreads, no Jah, no Rastafari,
No mercy, mercy, me, a stone's throw

From those poor folk with no temples
But the pillars that support the overpass,
Under a starlit roof named after gods.

Diderot, One

Had nothing to do with Cicero,
Allegro or Negro, so I summon Mango,
Mandingo, tango, Shango, call,
Nay, summon, my Uncle Joe,
Whose panegyrics grip, gyrate me,
Let me go, wound string, tight spool,
My high speed aim for a redacted name.
No drink to twist, smoke to turn
My head towards that particular sun.
Work my fingers to the bone
Until my thumbs lose their print,
Sunrise and dusk land on a line
I walk sideways, look askance.

> *Hear Aunty Bess, hear Aunty Bess,*
> *Hear Aunty Bess a holler;*
> *What she a-holler, what she*
> *A-holler, what she a-holler for?*

This skin school where we must all
Play fools just to get by or die,
Heroes in early graves marked
By an absence of headstones.
The books say the brave die young.
What they do not say must be found.

> *Oh Lord, me bucket got a hole*
> *In the center, and if*
> *You think I telling lie,*
> *Push your finger.*

After Horace

They say the blind feel out
What they see.

Think of Gloucester,
Eyes traded for insight.

But hungry belly alters
20/20 hindsight.

My birdfeeder designed
For Hummingbirds,

Sports red syrup and nozzles
Shaped for knitting-needle beaks,

Chestnut-sized sticklers, to tread
Air and syringe away.

This time, soup kitchens
Filled to capacity, turn away

More hungry than they can
Accommodate, more among us

Running on empty, some of us
Stuffed so full we cannot see.

Before Ovid

Change or die made me choose
My skin, a watertight suit
Zipped from head to foot,

Whose clasp I merely pincer
Between thumb and index finger
To undo history of –

And step away from –
As one might shun a nest of vipers,
Asleep in the shape of a jar.

Sappho, Oh Sappho

Danced on coals after the fire
Died and light started on the horizon
After a night of dancing around a fire

She lay with more than one head
Beside her belonging to more women
Than those she called lover or sister,

Some were cooks, some sang or played
Instruments, others just looked good,
All left it to her to say what this meant

For the city behind battlements ripe
For an invading army to plunder
Just as that fire reduced to ash

But not without fighting words
From this woman put to music
And choreographed for a troupe.

Aeschylus

The gift came in the post.
The post arrived in my sleep.

I woke with the package in my head,
On the nib of my tongue, fingertip,

Gift asked me to clear a moment
Before breakfast, grab this look,

No more than an eye-corner glance.
Could I say no to a surprise gift?

Africa

Skull for a continent,
baobab tree cradled,
rocked by a hand none
can see, palm pressed

small tamarind back,
urges me on, find something
I know nothing about, that trips
off my tongue as much as

off my hips, things to make me
go ah, think I have peacock eyes
behind my head, a fantail speckled
with eyes tripped by mist, light,

taste glands on my bare soles,
Nile in these veins, Sahara skin,
Gold Coast fort flesh; knock,
on wood, on bone, tap my spine,

needle pores, Africa, what *you*
is to me but some part in waves,
crease in mud, B's door
imperceptibly ajar, let me in.

Milesians

Not far from here, mist thrown from hilltop to deep valley,
from capital to border crossings, posted sentries; tunics,

shields, helmets, togas, head-in-cloud dreams,
cloud shapes, heads drift away from sloped shoulders

towards Athens, Rome, where books and fiddles scream,
burn, where fire toys with men, women, children, flora, fauna.

Heraclitus Meets Parmenides Meets Empedocles

1
Chaos, zigzag rain paints disused
shed window, cracked, polished,
sees in or out, framed by downpour
searching glass for portals, porters,
pores. There is language in this rain.
There is no word for race.
Rain without any history
I care to name or can name
out of care. Something happens to skin
that listens to water, amounts to more than...

2
A principle is a principle,
so says the Englishman without a hat,
under a noonday tropical sun,
in his wild search for an establishment
that serves a good cup of tea,
he believes will cool him down,
by working up a fine sweat on his brow;
all he needs is a breeze to crown the scene;
all he gets is a cold sweat when that sun dips,
lengthens his shadow, sets.

3
Air, my messenger.
Water, my consumer.
Earth, between my toes.
Fire, in my earlobes, taste buds.

Carry me quartet,
till kingdom come to town;
contain what's left of me;
consume me when I am dead.

Protagoras

There is nothing to say that the gods exist or do not
which is to say that the temples may be built on
sand rather than rock. Take time to carve your
initials in an apple-shaped lifelike sliced life.
There is nothing to say that the gods do not
exist or that they do, yet they may take exception,
in fact do, to your devotion to another living thing,
my point, since lightning must strike you, live your life.

Socrates Plato Aristotle

1

Talked himself into a corner and a sacrament
he considered a blessing in heavy disguise.

Walked into a mountaintop mine with the disposition
of a canary on the up and up, whistle stop.

Could not see his hand, his face in black raiment,
dark being thick rock, rock that left him bruised.

2

Is not to be confused with potato,
though both have skins that a lash might peel
and a stroke of love might heal.

Is not to be confused with plate
near empty for the hungry
brimful for the rich.

Is not late too little too late,
as in, she is late this month,
or fame came too late for Rhys,

for Lear, to appreciate it, when
Gloucester said, I see you.
Not Pluto, demoted to a rock.

May as well stick with a cartoon dog

3

Poor found a stage for a home,
house without a roof,
theatre with eyes for windows,
for looking in, plucked, not out,
and a doublewide porch for a mouth.

Archimedes

Stop me if light bends in water and shapes the window I look through
At a pond of light, glass where I see my reflection staring back at me.

Stop me before dust mars my sight as I pivot between the thing under
My nose and that far off, rain-full, dimple in earth, mirror for one
      sky after

Another curved sky, when the string that joins us, elastics too thin,
      breaks
Points of light, to send me reeling into dark, and you left to track my
      scent,

Where I cannot find you even if I could fit pieces whole again, no
      seam.
My footprints on water, your fingers on the wrong side of a pane my
      face

Almost touched, water-skin-punctured, backbone-bend-of-light
      entry,
For all to see who look with one eye above and one below the surface.

Hellenists Versus Hedonists

Wherever I hang my hat that's my home,
We are the wild boys, the fast boys
Assuming there isn't a rope around my neck
The flash boys, we are the boys the girls
And that hat on my head hangs just so.

    Call nasty, we make our mothers cry.

The ones who lived and the ones who died;
The ones who laughed and the ones who cried.

I need a hat stand and a hall for that stand.
We rejoice in our bad times and regret our joys.
A hat maker and tailor with clothes to match
We cannot know peace and know old is not for us,
My hat, and a barber to keep my head trim.
We are the wide boys who welcome the grave.

The list lengthens into conquest of a region.
We make children and never become fathers
My stay lengthens into the resistance to my need
We make love and never know solace
For a Spivey hat and all those trimmings.

    We live as wide boys in malls, content.

The ones who lived and the ones who died;
The ones who laughed and the ones who cried.

Cynics & Skeptics

1

What I see with my jaded eyes
tells me nothing about my heart

just as what I feel tells me nothing
about what I profess to see

the hand is quicker than the eye
I do not know for sure what I think

I think I know my mind until
I see dew lit on morning stone

2

I feel what I see and try to think differently
about both nerves and eyes,
one hand in the hot tub, other in the snow.

I smell my past when I glimpse cut grass.
Or is that the other way around?
Fill in (using a 2b)…

I know there is a trade route
that leads from my life now
to my first death way back when.

Epicureans & Stoicism

1
Left to hang out and dry on a clothesline,
her separates dipped in a salt marsh, fingernails
pared down to the quick and beyond the quick,

2
for that half-moon glow, that beaded blood
look on fingertip as if metatarsal
struck matchstick self to sprout red, wet flames.

Romany

Asked for an earthquake
got a tsunami

asked for fire and brimstone
got water searching for a home

asked for sun and got rain,
for nothing begets nothing in return

asked for a toga, a toga is not enough
without underwear,

nothing more than a sheet folded
hospital corners around bony skin,

blood rage in homeless circling
satellite HIV body.

Plotinus

Three-layered wedding cake
crowned with a couple whose lowest layer
a miniature hand scrapes for a taste
before that couple steps off their pedestal
to slice that cake for houseguests
as that child pivots hands behind back
face covered in telltale crumbs of who me, not me.

Catholics & Jews

1

Drank the blood of mine enemy,
tasted a morsel of his flesh
and called him Saviour, Father to me.

What to do with his bones?
Hollow them for a flute, eke out a tune
for a living, made so it tugs

purse strings of souls gathered
under one roof with a steeple
aimed at outer space where

God (it's a *g-thang*) hides His face.

2

It isn't the hair
It isn't the land
It is the hair
On a plait of land

It isn't the part
On the scalp of the sea
It is the part
Played by the sea

Of obedient hair
On a willing head
Of an element
Lighter than air

It isn't the hardship
Of a thousand years
It is those years
Rock-hard shipshape

St Benedict

This is how we roll: in flaxen robes, hooded,
room in the sleeves to fold our arms.

We chant what we keep
close to our chests: a hand dealt us
what we must play, never mind
our daze, bluster, grace.

Welcome, sit, eat what we eat,
sing if you find what we say moves you,
whatever, you will, like yesterday, find us
here tomorrow, and the day after that,

all's the same with us or without
us, in our circle, or lost someplace
outside it, for it cannot be named,
help us look for a song you can sing,

have a bite, a little something to chase it
down, not to mention a bed for the night.

Gregory The Great

Axe in one hand splits heads
text in the other hand parses syntax,
sorts woods from trees,
meaning in a mushroom grove,

umbrellas
for a picnic,
inhale,
nibble;
sip, swallow,
take notes.

Mushrooms so big
Greg shelters under them
from a thin rain sweetened
some, by falling through
sieves of honeycombs.

Was there ever human so torn
between apparent opposites
who made a reversible garment
from the two for all seasons?

Dark Ages

Cupped
candle

                flame

                wind bundles

before   armies
                invade

     bringing thunder
without
lightning
dead

                flame followed

by its   after
                glow

                empty upturned

        rigormortis
hands   curl

        fingers
harvest
battlefield
bones

Islam

1
I used a scythe to cut a star
from a sky full of such fruit

found that the more I cut down
more fruit lit up on that sky tree

2
de man can talk de man can think
de man use up nuff black an blue ink

de man spin plates balanced on rods a dozen
plates on a dozen rods

they can't stop talk we won't block ears
just as plate-spin keeps us all eyes

Hannibal

Crossed the Alps.
Did he hypnotize
elephants to believe
they were mountain
goats on a mission?

They say elephants
remember everything.
They say from that day
all elephants nose
their way across,

from this world
to the next, from
this flesh to that nether
body, akin to phantom
limb memory.

The Alps should have
Known better than
To cross Hannibal.

St Thomas Aquinas

Is there a pig more beautiful
than the lucky swine complimented

by Aquinas as godly, equal in said eyes to every
living thing, great and small, upright or on all fours,

on land, in sea or air, whispered so that the pig
must have felt Aquinas' breath on her

sow's ear, warm, urgent, incontestable exhaled truth
independent of understanding, immediately after that

compliment, seeped in one ear and out the other,
shipped off to market, to market?

Franciscans

If I sing unevenly
If I draw friendly fire
Draw blood from a friend

Take my hand
Think of my tongue
As doing no more

Than the following

Daily pull bucket from well
For one watersong
After another

For I will be one
With my split tongue
Bucket tied to well

Renaissance

Give me a pig-foot, a cockspur, a bell,
three cockleshells, and a bottle of your finest.

No bread, no water. Give me a drum,
a scrum, a song and dance, a rap, tap, rat-tat-tat.

No vaccines, no antibiotics. Give me life.

Me, no self, not I, just exploded lil' ole me
and mistress, Mrs. Jones.

Galileo's Snowflake

Burst from a pillow fight, high up out of sight, earshot.
Jar we're in, air so still, for this flotilla in straight lines,
No curlicues, no twirls in front a mirror, just up down,
But so very slow, it might as well be a sideways thing,
To stack imperceptibly, hand-over-ears muffle
In a library of powder, onion layers, skin on skin,
Keeping the world tucked in, underground,
Buried without bearings, we listen hard
For the start of this brittle splinter of glass
Strands on a head of hair made entirely of glass
Sprinkling almost-notes, more than halfway there,
Plastic crinkle mixed in whispers, sand-coated wood,
Until these bubbles we cannot see form an orchestra
For bubbles born and bubbles dying, us humans extra.

Machiavelli

The enemy of my enemy is my friend,
      the friend of my friend is no good to me if he is not the
          friend of my enemy

      The deal is, you take this beating heart and make of it what
          you will;
in return, when you give it back to me

at the end of your long and prosperous
      journey – what length, what prosperity – I do with it as I
          please. What's not to like?

Erasmus

Now you see me, now you
choose not to and so don't.

Why do you still search?
I have told you everything

I know you need to know,
about me, what I do not

know, you do not need, if you find
what you seek your life will turn

sour like milk left out too long,
you cannot see it turn bad,

unless you take my mood
for milk, as something you

should not stare at, but glimpse,
unless you are me.

More

Or less with less as more,
he is blessed who sees the score
etched on tablets in the sky,
light as cirrus tiptoeing by,

able to ride lightning
down to earth, full of thunder,
replete with dirt.

More is less without a home
More is ash in fire and brimstone.

Need I say, need less, is more.

Reformation

All things
polished

prismatic

creatures
caged

or free range

all things
cracked

turned dingy

history
ours

made them small

Burton's Anatomy

The hipbone connected to the thighbone
The thigh connected to the knee
The kneecap connected to the shinbone
The shin connected to the foot
The sole peeled from the foot

The hipbone connected to the backbone
The back connected to shoulders
The shoulders connected to the arms
The arms connected to the hands
The lifelines peeled from the hands

The hip connected to the back
The back connected to the neck
The neck connected to the skull
The scalp peeled from the skull
With a blunted instrument

Slavery Intro

Cup candle against a shower of arrows
carry that flame by eating the wick
with a lick and a spit from parched lips

coddle a flame burgeoned by a candle
waxed by the smelt by the melt of the dead

My skin for a lamp skin pores for eyes,
tremble fine hairs on skin cupped by eyes,
singed from staring down fire too long

from standing too near flame salt lick
for smell for heat as my eyes burst

butterflies their flung bedspread
far double wide, no pink slip nor moon glide
oh me, oh my, exploded long gone,

no soul, but two nailed to my feet,
no spirit, fermented blood, wafer flesh.

Come again, on a train I hold together
welded carriage to carriage,
on two sleeperless tracks, unparalleled,

who cups a candle against, not for,
always against, some thing or other.

Tidal

1. After *The Duchess of Malfi*

Long before I meet my end in that Robert Browning poem
As that creepy Duke's last wife, her laugh is mine, her gaze
Too, eager to take in all things. The artist who worked on me
Saved what the Duke threw away. I dodge him by going back
In time to earlier and earlier examples where people like me,
Who left this world without proper names find our lives
Footnoted in ruminations on their greatness by others
In church registers, court records, witness accounts back,
Back to Gilgamesh whose cuneiform mimic our bones.
Our bodies in that story, our breath a chorus of readers,
Touch of their touch, eyes laid on us, picked up by sight.
Us two joined, taken out of time, place, flung into space.

2. (Gravesend, Kent, 19 February 1603. Frances, the mulatto, was buried.)

Man, woman, or child,
The record says you died
That you lie in Gravesend,
Literally, your grave, your end.
I feel rude to do it but I must
Call on you, call you up
To help me in my need
To know more about you.

Man, woman or child,
You must stand now for all three:
Man and woman and child.
I need all of you to help me
Come to grips with a time
That had you cut out for labour,
Until you dropped dead
And your soul flew up

Above Gravesend,
Kent, Dover,
For Africa
Where your story
Begins.
Your cradle.
Our civilization.
Us burning the candle at both ends.

3. Dear Mary Shelley

I scramble your Frankenstein. Lift him from the
Of his science lab. He had a heart before he was born,
Switched off the moment he rolled me from that stone slab.
He tilts towards me and I catch him as he tips forward.
We dance like this, me grappling with his weight.
He holds on, looks tipsy he's so awkward, and we move
Back earlier, two of us now, not just me, another version
Of what happens to someone like me, this time black man,
Black woman, black child in a court record, a church register
Someone's will, if not Pepys' Diary. Ever been to the doctor
And have someone answer all the doc's questions for you,
Telling the doc where, what, and how you feel, tongue-tied?

4. Mayday, Liverpool.

A good day for a parade: sun and cloud
Taking turns to sweep the sky.
I march to drums, walk in dance steps
All the way from Toxteth Library
Down to the docks where I dipped
My feet in the Mersey to school them.

Limbo dancer limbo for me
Under the deck and over the sea

The drums shipped me back to Africa
The dance held me in its sway
I dipped my feet in the Pleiades,
Swam among the Atlantic drowned
Thrown overboard off seventeen thousand
Voyages in the Middle Passage.

Limbo dancer limbo for me
Under the deck and over the sea

5. Dreamboat

My friend Julian built a boat in his living room.
Said he would sail it on the river.
Took months of coming home from work
To launch his project. Saw it take shape
As if moulded from water, mini Ark, budding belly.
At last he applied the finishing touches.
Found he could not navigate it through
That front room window. So he removed
Said window. Friends helped him
Walk his craft down to the edge of the sound,
A quiet stretch near Greenwich.
He got in and pushed away into the deep
Lane and soon other boats showed up,
A tug, a barge and the surf they stirred
Almost sank him. He hurried back
To shore and picked more quiet
Times to go back to the element he loves,
Happy in his homemade boat.

6. For the Record

Caliban never had it so good with the crew on his island,
On his terms with his name and his words in Prospero's book.
Ask him what he said and how he said it before he met Prospero.
He raids a continent for it to operate his vocal chords.

I ate root bulbs, drank from the swan-necked flower, scratched
My back against the bark of trees, whistled in reply to feathered
      glories;
Howled with baboons at the sight of a hyena tricking lunch
From a lion and the lion too lazy to put up a fight.

He looks up and reads cloud cover for hide and seek
Between sun, moon, stars, river turning over a new leaf,
Sea at the promontory folding volumes of laundry,
Waves flapping their mouths in the breeze.

7.

(St Clement Danes, London. 21st December 1675.
Baptism: Charles, a black, his name Hercules)

Assume that he earned his name
with hard labour and matching physique;
that he had to be saved from himself;
rescued from his dark origins;
that his black skin needed to be cleansed;
that he wanted this blessing
more than he wanted to be free.

Assume one or more or all of these things
on behalf of a man who lost his tongue,
who counts on you for the righteous
in his name and bearing.

8. Unofficial Lido

My brother Andrew
and three friends
all in their teens
swam in the river
at Deptford
beside Pepys Estate

The trick was to stare
into the murk as if Thames
Tyne or Mersey
were outer space
pinpoint where wharf logs
jutted and where room trembled
free of splintered wreckage
for a clean dive

And in they went
one after another
entering clean and right
away swerving up
to avoid the shallows
emerge wide-eyed
with a whoop and a yelp
crawl back
up the jetty careful
not to cut themselves
on rotten wood
shaken and stirred
by the river readying
themselves swapping
versions of what took
place in front of each
other as they queued
for one more dive

9.

(Tyeburne tree, London 6th March 1663
A Negress or coloured woman hanged)

Black woman hold the city
as a lover would sans pity

For the city needs clothes and food.
The city is strange and misunderstood

Black woman hold the city
as a mother would her baby

For the city needs flesh and blood
The city is strange and misunderstood

10. Big Data

It was community
TV meets poetry
in a Words on Film
extravaganza
from Equiano to the present

The Beeb coughed up
enough for us to rent a river
boat, DJ thrown in
for good measure
sail from Westminster pier
to Thames Barrier
and back

I mean through that nest of shark
fins unimpeded
a truckload of black people
dancing to DJ tunes
spun to keep dance floor full

All you had to do was stand
there and let the current
work your hips
side to side
hold tight as tight can
to the nearest somebody
and in good time feel
that boat and all its cargo
spin out the barrier
one way and back in

another with hardly
a roil heave or riff
in the current below
Marley's One Love
never sounded sweeter
than that October
night on that
compound-free water

II.

*(Stepney London and Commissary Court, London, 1632.
Grace, a Blackamoor presented by churchwardens for living
incontinently with Walter Church, Stepney.)*

Walter promised me a warm bed
food and his unwelcome attentions

I promised him nothing

At first we slept back-to-back
and in our sleep we turned to face each other
hugged for warmth I believe

The utility of a hug grew into something sweeter

I referred to him as Unwelcome Attentions
from that day to our last together

They dragged me
into their court

said I sinned

He stayed out
of the frame

They said my
crime was that
I slept with him

not his for inviting me

If only I could wash him off my skin
I would wash myself clean down to my bones
But he stays with me after soap and water
his smell and his embrace
his breath
rapid as his body tightens and he says
Girl I love you
Stay with me
And I say
Thank you Unwelcome Attentions
and we fall asleep back-to-back
wake in a full embrace

Francis Bacon

No relation to pig, to sty, to trough, to mud, to slavery,
to market, to market.

No friend to the foe, of the fee fi fum.
No enemy to the beast of the Easter bun.

No relation to nation, to nacho, to macho.
No friend to fee, no fi to foe, no fum.

To market – tek ram ot
No cab sic an rf

Heads, Hobbes; Tails, Descartes

1. Heads

Cat nights and dog days dog chases tail
cat coughs up hairball

lady gives a damn man walks into bar minus one plus two

Knick-knack, paddy-whack.
Pop goes the weasel. Chi-ching.

2. Tails

Who put de cart before de horse put de harness before de furnace
walled up with brick and concrete
after de factory gates closed for de last time in a mean time

but not him oh no not him no good boy-o worthless thing
that man kept himself warm
all winter curled up in an oven so that he could think tanked straight

Spinoza

Wanted more from reality than a knife and fork carved up and
      served to him
mainly because he swallowed his food without chewing it or
      chewed sixteen times
for each mouthful, which turned food in his mouth
liquid then gas aka methane

Could be worse, could be gas you cannot smell and can see only as
      a side effect
too late to do anything about but lie back and observe it doing
      dirty work
somebody got to make
mess for everybody else to clean

Leibniz

Light poured from pint glass to pint glass as tea pours
from one cup to another held an arm's length to cool
pint glass drained by parent as tea is fed to baby

Never the other way around thank goodness
on a merry-go-round that spins too fast to hop on or off
where everything comes around twice

Baby laughs parents cry
dry eyes meet toothless wonder
hugs kisses make up sex

Liberals

Got it wrong
got it right
got it wrong again
until two wrongs
made a right

Never threw up
hands kept
those hands thrown
to the side for
balance stuck on

a fence until
name turned
from dirt to dust
to pollen riding
every insect wind

Locke Meet Hume

Slavery works so long as slaves do not know
the full extent of their condition

which darker skins prevent those slaves from ever
knowing as if reason were a membrane

unless black turns white and whites bear
black cross Ham curse skin of both impermeable to reason

as much as rhyme in his era and ours separated by a hair
whose ends split static fall hide behind teeth

Hume Meet Locke

Played the same unmistakable tune on a pennywhistle
hollowed bone from his enemy
spontaneity a tune that sounded like his instrument needed
an enema or his audience could use beeswax plugs for tin ears

two fish scales work overtime as covers for eagle eyes
and they do not fall no matter the time ozone

Romantics

1. Mary & Percy

Bombastic
as in da bomb

dream monster
machine desire

walked like one
talked like one

halfcocked on
cooked laudanum

doing things monsters do
being human

2. Byron

At the bottom of a pint glass is a carafe
out of which pours a string of octaves
measured up the joints of an index finger
knots of remembered bones for every conquest

At the bottom of every remembrance
is a carafe filled with some ferment
that whiffs of hope and despair in equal parts
down in one-be-merry head thrown back

3. Blake

Got his hands dirty
not just with lead ink

To illustrate my point
I ask all fathers

swallow a morsel
of the afterbirth of each newborn

you shoot up during a hey ho
sweet jesus come for me

4. Coleridge

Each day turns over a new leaf
eyes alone cannot tell

fog this morning on a roll
brought to the boil

by a sun climbing over hills
as much as clambering my skin

It's weather to be called away in
from a bed or desk to an errand

as one who leaves a cottage
in the middle of Kubla Khan

only to return to an absence
made by air with flesh not there

5. Wordsworth

I push through pebbles
my breath adds to what's here
I leave nothing behind me
that cannot be found later
what I chase remains hidden
with each step I might draw near
what keeps its distance
from me and multiplies with each step.

Pushkin

How far ahead of my time
can I get without losing
touch with both time
and my gunpowder self?

Answers by Thursday's last post
Please.

Take this drum
my dark skin stretched over wood for bone
tight so that insults bounce off
light sinks in

water-soaked drum
walking talking drum

ready for long nails fingertips feathers whips
not bullets

Answers by Thursday's last post
Please.

Rousseau

Vintage champagne bottle, candlelit dinner for two,
Corner of lazy eye catches harpist, heard, not registered,
back room of a mansion for a mind.

A meal for the age, where at least one hand clasps another,
no bed, empty, dead, for more than one night, no two
nights the same, till everyone wakes together,

time subtracted from some other soul, positively leaps
through fingers, so that body shivers, backtracks,
leapfrogs dazed, utterly alone.

Kant

Can
can't
won't,
can-can
tried to
failed
or failed
for want
of trying

Is every damn thing
going to be measured
against old man fat lady slavery?

No
yes
hell yes
well maybe

Hegel

Played the hole to Marx's bagel
so the ice-lolly stick joke goes

watched a mill next to a stream
saw a production line of automatons

who walked like children left to wander
little people who talked in tongues

made of lead laced with arsenic
forked and with a lisp

How wrong can you be about hot metal
pressed against flesh that brands a company

name on a body is not a question
so much as a formula from his time

down to mine and forwards into a black hole

I have seen things I cannot talk about
things I did that I am ashamed of

people I hurt whose names and faces
haunt my sleep and wake

though I profited from them verily,
thoughI gained nothing in the end

etcetera
just drink the damn poison and get

it over and done with for nobody listens
and somebody

the last body to leave
forgot to turn off the lights in a building

earmarked for cellphone captured
demolition

Equiano

Near water so much
it seemed you could absorb
water through your skin

For the strength of Samson
if black skin could outdo
hair of biblical proportions

Your book of exploits
made tea for two volatile
dispensed with table manners

One pull on the tablecloth
disturbs things set there
in one flourish

In a Durham Cathedral window
stained glass lauded troubled
cautioned against distress

But the two qualities in me
twinned as they are cannot be separated
in a photo finish or split by time

Schopenhauer

Think of something small
akin to loose change pulled
from a shallow pocket
with one foul scoop

Think of a glance
picked at picked out
piece by piece
from a wishing well

whose mirror never lies
whose glass wavers and stands
still just long enough
for a shadow to tiptoe across it

settle as if pooled for trust
negro trans on catwalk please
lower your face
drink your reflection

see how your shadow looks harder
than you and wonder how this
can be and you not be dead
on your feet buried standing

how ceilings become floors
made of glass or why that
glass reflects and is seen
through seen on all at once

Nietzsche

I pushed through turnstiles doubled
as revolving doors, stood shaky on discs
spilling blood, seasons, mass graves,
filled over slights, or gaze.

Not before I spit in my cold food
seated at a strange table, saliva stops
bullies from eating what's rightfully
mine, too late for this to be made better.

Take me to a nunnery where canticles
lull me into a stupor and the Super
wants nothing more than for me
to kneel before his raised overall.

Where my entire wardrobe is one
change of frayed hand-me-downs,
whose mirror tells me the same little
white lie as the day before I died.

Utilitarian

I knew a secretary
filed everything
carried a screwdriver
kept every screw
lined horizontal

wiped her office door
handle every morning
flicked off light
at day's end with her tongue
scraped squeaky clean

I knew her in the catholic sense
which comes as no news
is good news to no good boyo
she used me like her screwdriver
us two horizontal most times together

she called her privates her office door
I had to knock as if testing wood for luck
in our world one thing doubled as another
useful thing – stamen and proboscis
lights on for work off for a loosey goosey

Marx

South-East London surplus store,
near the Cutty Sark long gone now ,
where I found my pukka army fatigues
for a mountain hike on my red mountain
bike on a mountainous city rubbish dump

surplus store closed after a strike-turned-demo
led to a riot complete with Molotov cocktails
that made headway higgledy through the front
door letterboxes and fell plop on doormats
as plops turned into plots turned unseen

like milk into whoosh and the whole
story up in a flaming nest that climbed
ladders not for pulling up
to block followers but ladders
in stockings cut by a careless fingernail

Sojourner Truth

Pronounced artery in your thigh
you hang upside down as men cut
little trenches with penknives

cut until they open you up and I pour
from you by crawling over your body
turned upside down I pool under

your astonished head as some fool asks
what's happening they cut you loose
run from a disused warehouse

you pass out before you think tourniquet

I gather around you and try to soak back
inside your skin for clothing
you lie stock still for me but I congeal

with you in my arms our embrace across
two time frames rolled into one
for a measure no tailor can tape

Bergson

Ho, ho, ho,
ha, ha, ha, waving or drowning ho, ho, ho,
ha, ha, ha.

I look through the wrong end of a straw dipped in water,
a straw that bends in this light.

This is no laughing matter.
I look up the skirt of water when I should breathe.

My choice happens to be breathe or see.
I pick without thinking how light behaves

in the company of water, how
a flowing skirt allows me to see more than it wishes to hide.

Ho, ho, ho,
ha, ha, ha, waving or drowning ho, ho, ho,
ha, ha, ha.

Therapy for belly, ribs, jawbone, face, eyes
Narrowed by it, teeth bared for good.

Marie Curie

What is the language of rain?
Braille with a drum of fingertips
On my idling car as I wait for my son.
Rain excludes everything but tin-opener
Thunder, flexing all around.

All that's missing is lightning
For this posse to form, mount-up, head
Out, blaze a trail, sweep my car
Away with me unbuckled inside
Wondering what my son will think

When his yellow bus rumbles up.
But I am nowhere to be seen,
Not through this screening rain
Adorned with strokes of light,
Chased by cannon from a parade.

Douglass

Hair means something,
A conductor of charm,
Channels brain power,
Makes words static,
Bristle, charge, electrify.

Nose means a lot too,
For sniffing out
Change in unlikely places,
In the middle of a famine
In triplicate: eyes, tongue, ears.

Mouth moves according to body,
His four children,
His unschooled wife,
Feed his mouth.
His hair whitens, stands on end.

The man dances as well
Plays the fiddle, arm-wrestles.
History has no idea what to do with him.
He falls into so many categories,
He fits into none.

But the one with his name.
So praise him: His hair,
His nose, His mouth. Eyes
Thrown in for good measure.
Ears on the fella tuned all the time.

Tagore

Our driver sang Iqbal
As we wound up hill after
Muzaffarabad hill, until
Hired car sailed above cloud,

Into Kashmir, young men,
Salwar kameez flowing,
Ambling to the frontline,
Kalashnikovs slung on backs.

Flowers lined potholed roads.
Poppies blanketed fields.
Children raced after our car
Faces all teeth, saucer eyes.

Women swiveled, outsized
Bundles nested on their heads,
To follow our slow drive-by.
When we stopped, those hills

Turned some more, nothing
Like gyres, more a deep, planed
Blue cruised by cotton bales,
Occasional drones, rockets,

Kites at war, long tails, hint
Of razors. Our driver switched
To Tagore, love as earth axis,
Not hate, he intoned, yes, love,

Planted in every skull, Kashmir
Sun, so soft, people flock, stay.
Driver, sing us out of here or we
Never leave, Paradise, on earth.

Einstein

Epinephrine stick in my breast pocket
Nature in my face at my heels on my head
Stick above water not the same stick underwater
I wipe my shoes at front doors, hop over thresholds
Spirits follow in my wake into houses not homes
I mistake a hummingbird for a bee about to sting me
Same sharp pistons dice air with same velocity
This equation balanced on the stinking rose

Phenomenology

Being of sound mind and body
Doc's hammer hits my knee
and I kick involuntarily

an image of a lawn ripples
breeze that makes that neat green double
as sea, waves lined up offshore

I invite my skulking spirit, crawl
from under my goosed up skin
soak in this morning crisp

light baths a world
made for nothing until now
the furthest thing a mountain

range that keeps its brooding bulk
sixth sense that a wall braces sea
the fastest eagle rides currents

before it dips black and white helmet
towards me as I crane at this raft
all feathers and hollow bones adrift

smallest thing is a hammer,
aimed at my knocked knees
that give without warning

Levi-Strauss

Lego or plasticene? Lego and plasticene.
Onion or oyster? Onion and oyster.
Mirror or lamp?Mirror and lamp.

Mirror, polished or cracked?
Polished and cracked.
Genie in lamp or genie out for good?

Lamp in that beast.
Light that shows ways
There for the take.

Fanon

The colonial throws up
his hands, walks away
from you, me, one, all,
leaves behind, nothing,
but that colony of mind,
which happens to be man,
woman, child, just like those
dearly departed, but without
matter, and therefore no
backbone. They treat
my skull like a house.
They look at me, see
a dog, without a home,
minus a leash or micro
chip origin tracker.

Those same colonials
retire from my head
or I evict them, only
to see an aspect of me
legging it away from me,
as they take me with them,
the me I wish to parse from
myself for a purer version,
all this without me being
there, if such a move can be
pictured, in the colony
of my mind, without
calling in medics who
chase after me brandishing
my plantation name.

Barthes

Magazine shoots pot-bellied child, clad in flies,
wells for eyes, pained stare at my lens.

On the facing page, jump to ad of woman and man
scant clothes, nostrils flared, no luxury spared,

topless car for man, bonus young woman
for car upholstery, car more a four-poster bed.

In an ideal world where I want for nothing
there is not one thing for sale, no price for want,

no need for price, no top down, trickle clown
alms race, no streets overrun by rifles for cut flowers.

Though armed with the three P's, try as I might,
I cannot shake that starved child from my head.

W.E.B. DuBois

If ever we needed a relay to be run on behalf of a people
With the baton passed efficiently from hand to mouth
No cockups, no missing the receiving palm or dropping

Of said wisdom of history into oblivion, then this would be
My ideal lineup on lane two or three; not one, for that
Leads to complacency and invites crosshairs on the chest,

Leaves our man no option but to run out of the stadium
Far from the reach of sodium lights, beyond the noise
Of generators, to this other kingdom full of republics

Where hammocks suggest another measure for time,
Where sunsets resemble lavish holiday drinks
And a pillow means rice, equals a good night's sleep.

Malcolm

Second in line to DuBois, handover smooth,
Run more a glide of syllables at the Oxford Union,
Prayer just as liquid as his magnifying specs.

All the things he becomes step in to help him.
He grows old in front of his children and wife,
So old when he speaks we know what he will say,

Before he says it, and we agree wholeheartedly,
Without his assent. There comes a time when all
He needs to do is show up for good to break out.

MLK Intro

Homestretch forty years after felled on that balcony,
our unofficial president now on The Mall,
giant in stone, finish this race on a nonstop treadmill
bound for glory, if a safety cord exists, pull for engine stop
before we all trip and fall under strain, running on empty,
from fast asleep to wary wakeful, we juggle, while we eat
fire for three meals. You know that tape you breast is no end
just a false start, a new race, the same race by another name,
that's why I pick you, Malcolm, and DuBois, to run, who else
but you three on a comeback despite a violent finish, in a race
with no finish line, no end in sight, trusting someone will be there
without your need to say, take my outstretched hand before
both of us tumble and fail not just ourselves but all who follow us.

The Sirens' Song by Romare Bearden

Nikki's in the picture as I stand beside her
In the museum down the road from Maya's place
And see us two reflected in the glass over the frame
Or in the lights bouncing off the 'big men's colors'*
Of the rendition of Odysseus bypassing a port.

The black stick figures chiaroscuro à la L. S. Lowry
Except for the heraldic in the ordinary of black folk's
Extraordinary heraldry, our hero lashed to the mainmast
Sees and hears all and can do nothing about any of it
While his deafened crew rows away from temptation.

That is the story of our history if truth be told,
That we live and take struggle in our stride,
That the color of our lives may pass us by
If we obey forces besides love because want
Is our only compass and love our constant loss.

---

* 'Big men's colors' is how Bearden described the bold colors of his paintings.

Wilson Harris

Gone now, the way of mist
Over Kaiteur, falls above,
Cloud below, eye-twist,
Head-spin, death as love.

Gone from our skin school,
Wake chiseled on stone
We barefoot for its cool,
Flute carved from bone,

We pick up with our eyes
Lift, tilt, fill our skulls
For keeps, wonder why
Else but this push and pull?

Peacock tail spread...
Ladder waterfalls...
The pull of knowledge
The push of questions

We walked Georgetown,
Trench divided roads,
Seawall mud head frown,
Sombrero-sized toads,

Kite nosedive breeze
Flip cotton hem dress
Above bruised knees
Scrub floors or bless.

There is no time left,
Our talk just run out,
You gone, I am bereft,
Your words in my mouth

Jumpstart once more
Come back through
Turnstiles, take the floor,
I won't let go of you.

Dante

Not circles but squares drawn in sand.
A dry mango seed and barefoot hop
On one foot from square to square,

Kicking that seed from one to the next,
Keeping mango in the borders of squares
Until the legs burn from covering

So much ground on one foot,
Advancing one square at a time,
From the bottom up.

Pushkin Redux

Two lives for you,
A second chance,
Show your hand.

All you need do
Is par-tay; you dig?

In a time not yours
Far from your land.

The questions remains,
Is one life plenty
For us?

Anna Akhmatova

Stands in winter outside a prison.
Her son looks her way through bars.
His small window on winter;
Her dark figure against snow.
One among many mothers,

Wives who keep winter vigil,
She squeezes in her poetry between.
Her fingers numb, sight failing,
Son jailed for something she wrote,
Writing she could not help doing.

Lighthouse

Slick
Stretched
Waver
Over
Rock

My shadow harder than me
Walks on water

Vertical diver
Joins self
Fingertips first

Beacon call
Heartbeat summons

Cut deep
Dark pitched
Pegged to horizon

Land
End
Tower
Signals
Ships

My shadow swims away from me
Breaststroke breaks liquid skin

Bones scatter
Underwater
Road harvest

Ancestor bones
Too many to count

Road I walk
With gills
Lidless eyes

George Seferis

With seashell to ear,
An eye for every shell
Happened upon, sought,
Chased, on a balcony
Overlooking a square.

A fountain invites
Young and old to idle
For a cool breeze wet
By that artificial spring,
Seagulls shuffle on tiled

Roofs and wrought lamps,
Poised to swoop for crumbs,
If someone throws some
Thing worthy to stir and flap,
Beaks clawing the ground.

GS, cold sweat flowers
Your shirt, your noose
Handkerchief cannot
Stem rings that widen
At armpits and crotch.

Now you pick up a shell,
Lean your heavy head,
Press shell hard to ear
For the sound of the sea,
For the beat of your blood.

Lorca

Stands by a trench, his chest opens
To the aim of a firing squad.

He has no name when he falls
Among other young men.

His books run from him
To shelter among library shelves,

Where hushed tones and the odd
Chair scrapes on the wooden floor,

And versions of Lorca open gaps
On shelves and fill them back up.

Where the trench of spines
Packed in neat rows calls for

The steady fire of a gaze;
The sure gaze of fire.

Hitchcock's Vertigo

On their first date, after midnight,
He insisted they climb to the roof,
Up the rusty fire escape lashed
To the west side of a ten-story
Redbrick disused shed
So that they could view the city
As the city never wanted to be seen –
From its dying industrial backend.

Once there, she walked to the edge,
Sat, legs draped over the side. He
Stood, glued to the middle, unable
To budge. She spotted phosphorus
Adrift in the river, picked out by moon,
Scattered so, sky became a current
Steeped with stars dead long ago,
Funeral arrangements pending.

Aime Cesaire

Back to skin as a suit
Stitched by history,
By candle and moon.

Back to skin for a name
For the nameless ones
Who otherwise look

Beautiful, who share
One name for men,
Women and children,

The very old, the baby,
King and commoner,
The dead and unborn.

The same skin sings
As if held between lips,
Or if the tongue twisted,

Folded around air.
The same skin called
For freedom for all names

Walked away from bones,
From flesh, from blood,
Behaving like a kite

Cut from a long string,
Gripped by a black child,
A kite angling across fields.

Calvino

What did you mean by eponymous,
When you described that city on the hill
Modeled after a cloudscape, adrift,
Whose architects wore togas and crowns?

I've worn away the heels of countless
Practical shoes trying to find out,
My head tipped to receive the right signal,
Eyes glued to my feet, arms ready to break

My fall, steps without footfall, not gingerly,
With my inner ear cooking up the interior
Of a conch shell I need two hands to steady
As I pour its air into mine, so gravity whispers,

Much like turning a sock inside out and feeding
My foot into it so that it ends up around my foot
Right side out, no room left for air, fabric
For skin I can peel off and change at will;

Nothing like seeing the city from high up
Through a wine glass that turns the whole place
Upside down and miniaturised to grace
A nimble wrist, not dainty, too many veins,

Not dipped in any pond, and certainly not pale,
A wrist that invites my lips to the point
Where a butterfly appears trapped under skin
That's raceless, genderless, equal and true.

Our King James

C.L.R. in his rocker holding forth on Shelley
Who put the r in radical as much as the p.

At The Albany I raved with a master drummer,
Ballerina and light technician before a live
Audience of likeminded and polite souls.

Riding home from the all night workshop
In a city polished by sun, I opened the throttle
Of my 250 and sang to a four-stroke engine.

Those years lined up, hook and sinker, without end.
Time was a pulse, an ah, and a hum, picked up
In another's thighs next to my seashell ears.

I walked on air most days, and slept so sound,
set in threes, out of harm's way, rattled
Me awake for my shift, on locked Ward Five.

Martin Carter

Peered over the rim of his spectacles.
He knitted his brow.
He threaded his fingers in mock prayer.
The world map
Turned from red to brown to black
And blue, drained of empire.

Across the trench in the shantytown
Children race old tyres with sticks,
Washing sags a line strung from
Pillar to post, a ribbed stray dog
Forages, a child answers to his name

Called from a windowless frame
By a woman who issues a threat
About what would happen if she
Calls again, a cut-tail, a licking,
A curse and a blessing in disguise.

Maybe it was Martin's eyes, his stare,
That made the map lose its focus.
Mercator changed to Peter's
As his eyes swiveled from above
The rim of his specs to below.

Sargasso Sea

Antonio
Your sea of lentils
Turned over afterhours at the Lord Jeffrey
A prism at the bottom of a whisky

Rhys peered back at us
Beside her great house in ruins

It would take years for this
Stare down to dissolve
Make peace with broken glass

Smoothed by endless voyages
Their thrown silk of Africans

Forced to keep squid company
Bones returned to sand
Steps erased by waves

Our glasses raised to spirits
Islanded in attic and seabed
For a foolproof burn
Barefoot skip midday sun

Mandela

Made me believe in a salmon's waterfall climb,
Grizzly claws and jaws dodge, and spawn,
Where so many salmon spawned before.

Made me see the toot in Toots and the Maytals
When *I-and-I scene* enough for two lifetimes,
And the scales, the weighted scales, fell from my eyes.

Made me taste the just in justice, in coconut water
Offered lukewarm in the green nut, which his cutlass
Cracked in two while he held it, and I scraped jelly

Using a spoon carved by him from the husk of the nut;
He touched me and I had no idea until it dawned
On me that his bony forearm draped my shoulders,

Radius and ulna no heavier than scentless orange sun,
A messenger sun, chasing me on my morning run.

Diderot, Two

Did a row or two on Ocean
Drive in my dreams
Barefooted thru
Sand from gold castaway
By evolution
My back to the city
I steered – so it seemed
As I stared at containers,
Their neat stanzas straight
Out of Mandalstam,
Lined up, equidistant,
Offshore, in orderly fashion,
For a pew in the port,
One ship, a destroyer,
Whose grey camouflage
Made the sea change it's mind
From accommodation
To despair and then some,
And gather all the zinc roofs
Of shacks in nearby Liberty
City into one blinding flash
Raising water in my eye,
Until I looked away,
Marched away, back to
Another day, my back
To the sea, swell, shush,
The sea's reggae dance,
One step forward,
Two steps backward,
Inna Babylon.

Walter Rodney

Land of many waters
Flow from his pores

Land of seven peoples
Breathe through his skin

Walter at Speaker's Corner
Sundays practicing

All waters all peoples
Channeled this man

A stick bends in water
But does not break

A people grows as branches
On a tree with miles of roots

Walter not water
I wash my face and head

In your name
Refresh my time with yours

Cut short cut down
But the roots remain

And more trees
Spring up in your corner

More rivers branch out
More people arrive to hear

Faces open as the day
Yours met London

And liked what you saw
And saw what you liked

To take back home Including
groundings with brothers,

Sisters and a party to your name
But bombs stop flesh

While spirits branch out
Airborne and underground

Take root and prosper
Passed from hand to mouth

To heart to flesh and blood

Trans Coda

A boy posted on a boat at sea
This boy is and is not me
As his vessel dips towards
Curved horizons so curves
Rise and back away

Both keep their distance
On a table cleared of hours
Just two parts to the water
Days diving for coins
Nights seeing this zinc ripple

A dozen children in a hammock
Sing in a yellow submarine
Ropes creak and eat into posts
Of a house on stilts floors swept
By a grandmother's floor-length dress

Fresh bread every morning
A curried air most evenings
Lunchtime empty smell
Mosquitoes scoot for shelter
Rob that child of a prized halo

Yes to the alligator lodged across
Said trench and oops for bare feet
That stepped on what they took
For a log that shifted and reared
Making those feet cycle in air

I woke with all this and tried
All morning to shake it off
My head and still a part of me says
No I do believe what I remember
Yes I do not remember what I believe.

Yeats, Eliot, Pound

I roll up long sleeves
Dare to eat a kumquat
Tell myself, convert
Eyes to bifocals
Store other I in a briefcase
Limbo lower
Palms swing chariots
Stilts hoisted blueward
Brushes rinse sun
Catch rain
Bring beach sound
Marrow for my bones

Yesterday, I sent you
On an errand.
Eyes thrown over shoulders
For any trace of your return.
Tomorrow, promise me
You will not do the same
Thing before today runs out.
Handful of water I try to grab
But come up hands empty
Every time. Light I swipe my hat
To fill, only to pillow air.
Should I wait for the current
To smooth broken glass
On the beach or take a chance
And sprint, b-line, for the water?

He rolled. We shared a smoke
And a private joke. One about
Snake and mongoose. Both sly.
We went back and forth
In a calypso, he took up where
I trailed off in a singsong

That as we smoked grew
Raucous, tickled deep,
We must have seemed (to that group
Of clubbers dressed too sparse
For the climate and who hushed as
They sauntered past) a couple
Of giggling old queens.

DW

Channel Derek thus –
The bivalves of my heart
Jump for joy at the sight
Of lemurs crossing a jungle parapet
Baked with dew as they hold
Limbs, joined for upright balance
Weighed by light that scales
This jungle in a steeplechase
Without end, if the annals
Crafted by the ancients hold water
Rising from lemur instep
As if exhaled by a tired earth
Too long in a giving frame
Too much with hope that takers
Learn from breathing in
And might seek to even out
Things some, hand-in-hand,
Back scratch for back scratch,
Just as that light operates its trowel
So that what the earth gives
We gratefully receive and return
With interest in our children.

KB

Mike up Kamau so –
Bow to gods behind
Bulletproof glass
Sun breaks stones
Dashed at skin
Peeled from flesh
Shaken off bone,
Bow to oil tankers
Parked offshore
Beside bank account,

That part seawater
Erase international datelines
Pull umbilical chords from
Newborn countries
Till they snap
Back strap IMF
World Bank debt
Think oil tanker
Snap-chat or Instgram
Cut vocal chords
Now how, bowwow?

Uniformed guards trail me
At boutique malls
I breathe shallow
Square my shoulders
Against their hunch
Align my spine
With history lived below
Deck as much as above
The now in, now out, navel
Ready for cotton bud
Wielded by love.